The Sun Signs of Love... Sagittarius

By Derek & Julia Parker

tempo
books

GROSSET & DUNLAP
Publishers • New York

Contents

©Mitchell Beazley Ltd 1973, 1976
All rights reserved

ISBN 0-448-12348-7

First published in the United States
by Grosset & Dunlap, Inc.,
51 Madison Avenue, New York 10010

Derek and Julia Parker's
researches published in this book
accompany original material by them,
published in other works, which has
been re-edited for *The Sun Signs
of Love.*

The Sun Signs of Love features work
by the following artists: Ann Meisel, Diane
Tippell, Elizabeth Klein, Michael Embden.

Sagittarius in love

Traditionally, the Sign of the Hunter, Sagittarius, provides its inmates with plenty of strong hunting instincts. Not many Sagittarians may be whooping it up on horseback, but thousands express this powerful instinct in other ways—scrabbling around in piles of rubbish to find just the right piece of wood, toiling on an eternal quest for knowledge, or—of course—hunting for a mate. Soul-mate or bed-mate? Well, because of the Sagittarians' natural duality they need both from the same partner, though they often swing from one extreme to the other, either needing all sex or all intellect for equally long periods of time.

If, however, this dual need cannot be satisfied by one person, the free-ranging Sagittarian will have deep but separate sexual

and intellectual relationships with the opposite sex, hoping perhaps that the twain will never (or hardly ever) meet!

Sagittarians are highly sexed but generally speaking do not take relationships too seriously. However, their over-all attitude is highly colored by the position of Venus, the love planet. If it is in Sagittarius itself (see page 54), with the Sun, then the duality, plus all the fun and games Sagittarius can cope with, will be in evidence. If Venus is in Scorpio, a heavier, more emotionally oriented attitude is likely. In Libra, we find a far greater inclination to be romantic than most Sagittarians would care to admit to, but which is rather splendid for their partners.

The Sagittarian needs a great deal of freedom of expression and cannot for a moment tolerate a relationship that is claustrophobic or a partner who is possessive. Indeed, the need for freedom is so powerful that it can become a source of difficulty if the partner isn't considerate or broad-minded, especially after marriage.

Sagittarians are not difficult to please, and perhaps more than anyone else, are optimistic. They are enormously lively and enthusiastic, both in love and in their attitude to life in general, and it's not difficult to bring out this side of their personalities. When their response to some lively suggestion is not immediate, something is very wrong, for it takes a lot to get Sagittarians down. Most likely they are suffering from some small-minded person who cannot see the wood for the trees, or some dreary pessimist who tries to stop Sagittarius from positive and exuberant self-expression.

Dates with Sagittarians are usually happy, spontaneous affairs—a day at the races may well be suggested. Sagittarians love travel and any excuse to get into a car or onto a plane is seized, so if it can be afforded (or even if it can't) a quick flip to the nearest sunny playground may be arranged. The Sagittarian loves to gamble and may well spend an hour at a club or a casino *en route* to the airport—though conversely we have the really studious Sagittarian who will spend hours on end dragging a loved one round colleges and bookshops!

You and Aries

Gifts that are sure to please

When Sagittarius finds an Arian friend, it will soon be discovered that they live their lives at a very similar pace and can both become very enthusiastic about anything that inspires them. This really is a fun combination, and time spent together will be spiced with a great deal to make life worth while, memorable and amusing. Sagittarius will notice that Aries likes to be out in front in every conceivable way. But Sagittarians can hold their own, shooting off their arrows one after the other, always heading to where the last one landed but with their minds on where the next one is going. The main Arian fault is selfishness. Sagittarians are far more philosophical and can help prevent Arians from becoming impossible. Sagittarian and Arian friends will be seen every fine (or wet) weekend dashing off to some sporting event.

When a Sagittarian man finds an Arian girl, dressed no doubt in a smart red pants-suit, he'll inwardly give a little pony-like snort of anticipation of the good times to come, and go right up to her and start talking. She's a straightforward, pleasant, uncomplicated girl, and fairly passionate, too. She'll not worry about Sagittarius' other girlfriends; in fact, she'll probably have one or two strings to her bow herself. The affair may well be pretty hot stuff, and they'll both get much from from it. What is more, in this combination both will feel they can really be themselves. It won't be in the least necessary for either to put up any kind of facade.

When a Sagittarian girl finds her personal Arian Ram it won't be long before she finds herself trotting behind him into the nearest thicket! If Aries is a fast worker, so is she, and passion, real enjoyment of life and outings together will feature in this particularly happy period in their lives. She may come across Arian selfishness once in a while, but she is more than likely the type to have other dates to fall back on and won't take it too hard. It'll be a perfectly uncomplicated and enjoyable relationship.

When Sagittarius marries Aries both will throw themselves into the relationship with great enthusiasm, take up the challenge—and love every moment of it. Both types need a very strong element of freedom within marriage, and Aries mustn't be selfish about this, nor must Sagittarius take too much for granted. There won't be a moment's boredom, nor will the children have square eyes from looking at too much TV. Aries will keep them busy going to sports clubs and dancing lessons, and Sagittarius will soon be compiling library lists and making sure homework is completed!

You and Taurus

Sagittarius and Taurus are as different as chalk and cheese. Sagittarius is all go, mentally and physically; Taurus is static, taking life calmly, hating to be rushed, liking peace and quiet, never ever in a hurry to accept new opinions or change his or her mind. So when these two become friends they will find wide differences in their outlook and whole attitude to life. Can they learn anything from each other? Yes. And perhaps it's in this way that the friendship will cement itself in the first place. The bright and breezy, sporty side of Sagittarius would be the least likely to appeal to Taurus, though if we use the word "sporty" in its literal sense, they could of course enjoy joint sporting activities. More likely, though, Taurus will admire Sagittarius when he or she is in a studying mood, wanting to learn more and more in greater and greater depth about a subject, for Taurus doesn't have the urge to be an eternal student, like Sagittarius. More socially, both Taurus and Sagittarius have pretty hearty appetites and like food and company, so this is common ground.

When a Sagittarian man finds a pretty, slightly chubby Taurean girl, they'll both be in clover as he declares himself, quietly and gently but passionately, with perhaps the help of a bunch of violets. But we must remember that, of all the Signs, Taurus (apart from having the reputation of being the best-looking) is the most possessive, and this could cause clashes between you. You *cannot* be possessed, and will have to make

Gifts that are sure to please

sure that she realizes this. She's slow to be sexually aroused, but passionate. A pleasant affair—but get your varying attitudes properly sorted out.

When a Sagittarian girl finds her wavy-haired Taurean man she must remember that he's far more conventional than she, and could indeed be quite shocked by her love of freedom. If he's very young, he may not say so; but it's nevertheless possible that he may well feel that "a woman's place is in the home". (She won't, for certain!) They'll have a lot of fun, of course, and she could find that she's put on a pound or two around the hips because of additional meals out—and good ones at that. But, Sagittarian filly, you're not to be possessed, and you must make quite sure he realizes this.

Sagittarius must make allowances for a much slower Taurean pace in life. Taureans may not grasp ideas, situations or projects nearly as vividly or broadly as Sagittarians, though on the credit side they're very sensible and more constructive, with a determined, plodding attitude which doesn't come easily to Sagittarius. In marriage there will be various positive qualities which will blend.

You and Gemini

Gifts that are sure to please

Sagittarius and Gemini are opposites across the Zodiac, but, while they have many opposing characteristics, there is a natural rapport between them. A Sagittarian will always be able to "see what a Geminian is getting at", whether they actually agree or not. Astrologers use the word *polarity* to describe these interesting characteristics. It's a good thing for Gemini to have a Sagittarian friend. It's a good thing for Sagittarius too, but Gemini will gain most from the combination, with Sagittarius on the whole doing the hardest work! This won't mean digging in the garden or washing the socks, it will mean that Sagittarius will be *teaching*, having a deeper, more meaningful mental outlook. Both types are renowned for their duality, for doing more than one thing at a time; both are also rather restless, and when together could catch this quality from each other. But how stimulating they will be for each other, too! Perhaps, for instance, Sagittarius will be learning a language and will persuade

Gemini to follow suit (though Gemini is rather prone to crazes, and study may not last long).

When a Sagittarian man finds a lively, light-hearted, flirtatious Geminian girl he must remember that she's not usually a very passionate type. To know a little more about the balance between passion and affection in her, see pages 54 and 60 and the positions of Mars and Venus at the time of her birth. If she has Venus in Aries she'll be more passionate; if in Taurus, slower to arouse; if in Gemini, very flirtatious. But he'll probably have the experience to cope with all this, and while he could find her just a little cool (though not unfriendly) they should enjoy life a lot. She's not possessive, and will take her love life even less seriously than he does. He'll have plenty of rivals, and won't mind because he'll have other girlfriends too.

When a Sagittarian girl meets a lively Geminian, she'll find he's one of the most approachable guys ever. She'll only have to phone him on a very slender pretext and they should be talking for hours. He's intellectually and emotionally a light-weight. Her fiery passion will be ahead of his, for he'll always question himself about his emotions. But he'll respond well to her, and as time goes on she'll find that there's a strong element of real friendship in the affair. He'll be inquisitive, fun, will challenge her broad over-all statements and, as far as sex is concerned, will like plenty of variety and change.

No problem of communication in a Gemini/Sagittarian marriage, for this couple will never stop talking, even in their sleep!

You and Cancer

"Don't fence me in" is a Sagittarian theme song, for this Sign is the most open-air loving of all twelve. On the contrary, Cancer is the most claustrophobic, so other friends will raise an eyebrow at a Sagittarius/Cancer partnership, for they really couldn't be more different. Sagittarius will scream for fresh air (psychological as well as physical) when a situation becomes at all claustrophobic; while Cancer will want to feel protected by sound psychological walls (a defensive shell, if you like), as well as needing plenty of roots to give a sense of security. These types can work happily together through some sort of study project—perhaps involving history, a favorite Cancerian subject. But they do need *something* to work on together; then, when Sagittarius is ready to take up the challenge, Cancer will help him or her to stay with it to the end. If they both like sport, they will get together happily when swimming—but even on the beach a difference will crop up—Sagittarius loving to sunbathe, and Cancer not being able to bear too much Sun!

When a lively Sagittarian male meets a Cancerian girl he should try to hold back and *not* behave in his usual extrovert way. She will like a delicate approach, and he should be all sympathy and kindness if when at first he asks her for a date she is afraid she cannot fit it in. He'll have to be patient. She's a girl of terrific moods, and can change quickly. She's a great romantic,

Gifts that are sure to please

and very often as soon as she's involved with a man she begins to think in terms of marriage and starting a family. It's here that Sagittarius should be really careful, for she's very clinging and this could put him off. She'll be a bit lighter-hearted in her attitude to men if Venus was in Gemini when she was born (see page 54).

When an energetic Sagittarian girl finds a nice, kind, quiet Cancerian man she should ask herself carefully, before giving him a come-on, if she wants at this particular point in her life to be protected and looked after. Perhaps she does; it could be a delightful change if she has recently been entangled with a nonstop Arian. However, if she wants to continue enjoying life and love in a lively, not-too-serious way, she should be careful, for Cancer may well be thinking of the long-term future. If she wants to go ahead, she could ask him (and other friends) to dinner, and cook a classic fish dish. He'll love that.

Sagittarius and Cancer in marriage must remember that their basic attitudes to marraige and to children will really be very different. Cancer is very prone to worry, and Sagittarius can help here, having a philosophical and optimistic outlook.

You and Leo

Gifts that are sure to please

In spite of the Leonine reputation for being pompous, "snooty" and regal, one mustn't forget that the ruling planet of Sagittarius is Jupiter—king of the gods. And that is why Sagittarius and Leo hit it off so well: it's very easy for Sagittarians to identify with the Leo splendor and dignity. Jupiter was always after the women, up to all sorts of fun and games—one moment a shower of gold, the next a fly. And perhaps that's the real Sagittarius, too—the side of Sagittarius to appeal to Leo, who, when he or she catches a Sagittarian friend in a lively, extrovert mood, will be ready and eager to let down the mane and join in the fun. Together these two really have the knack of enjoying themselves. They are both optimists of the first order, both enthusiasts, and whether poring over Leo's latest masterpiece or Sagittarius' latest philosophical novel, they will love every precious moment they spend together.

When an informal, casual Sagittarius man is attracted by a Lioness, it's possible she may not think too much of him at first—a bit *too* informal in his appearance, a little *too* casual in his approach. In other words, he won't be giving her the full regal treatment which she may well have come to expect from previous lovers. But give her time, and she may soon discover that there's a great deal more to him than meets the eye. She'll love the more serious, philosophical side of his personality. She'll also love—and identify with—his sheer enjoyment of an enthusiasm for life in general and love in particular. So once Sagittarius has broken through any early barriers, and assessed how affectionate she may be from the Sign Venus was in when she was born (see page 54), they will be set to hit the high spots. She will put him up on a pedestal, for while there's something of the princess about her, she's also a willing slave to those she really admires.

When a Sagittarius girl finds a Leo man she may soon realize that he could be rather more conventional than she, and may like a fairly formal approach. He's not the sort to be affronted by being approached by a girl—it'll flatter him—but if she decides to throw a party it might be a good idea if she wrote him a formal invitation. He'll admire good organization, so if she's wise she'll allow herself plenty of time to get the food ready, and will blossom forth in a stunning new purple gown. Remember one word when he's around: elegance.

Joint rulership must be the theme in a Sagittarian/Leonine marriage and Leo must accept Sagittarius' need for freedom without getting too stuffy about it.

You and Virgo

There are some striking differences between Sagittarius and Virgo, but intellectually they can find a great deal of common ground. The Virgoan mind is tidy, analytical, inquiring and adores minute detail. Sagittarius' mind, on the other hand, is broad, perhaps rambling and rather disorganized, but very good and very profound. So it's easy to see that a Virgoan friend can fit very well indeed into the dynamic Sagittarian scheme of things. Putting it bluntly, Virgo will come along behind and pick up the pieces, tidy the loose ends and fill in all the gaps Sagittarius may leave behind! Both are energetic types, and may well find they share sporting interests—cycling, walking, athletics, all are very much part of the scene for both of them. In this particular combination we have, too, quite possibly some pretty powerful literary potential: a great number of novelists are

Gifts that are sure to please

Virgoan, and there's many a Sagittarian writer (and publisher, too). Joint interests should be developed, especially if they either broaden the Sagittarian or Virgoan mind . . . or narrow their hips! Physical exercise is essential for both Signs: it can help Virgo lose nervous tension and refresh Sagittarius when tired by mental exercise.

When a Sagittarian man is attracted to a Virgoan maid, looking ever-neat in her navy and white, he could be a little put off by the air of *purity* that will amost inevitably surround her (so contrary to the Sagittarian scene!). However, getting to know her, he'll realize that any shyness is genuine and sincere, and this, too, will appeal to him. He must be patient, and it will help him a great deal to know what Sign Venus was in when she was born (see page 54). She'll warm to him most readily, and easily, if it was in Leo. She could well have a few psychological battles to fight if it was in Virgo, for she'll be rather critical of her lovers and may find fault with them, thus making problems for herself. However, Sagittarius, if he adopts a kind, enthusiastic but not gushing attitude towards her, could help overcome any difficulties.

When a Sagittarian girl is attracted to a Virgoan man things may not be too easy. She must remember he'll be rather fussy, even "old womanish", in some ways. His pad, for instance, will be very neat indeed. She shouldn't find it too difficult to stimulate him, intellectually at any rate; sexually, she may have to bide her time.

Sagittarius can certainly soothe the Virgoan nervousness and tendency to worry in marriage. But Virgo must try not to be too fussy, or to nag, as this could mar the relationship. Let Sagittarius help develop pure warmth and affection within the slightly cool Virgoan heart.

You and Libra

Gifts that are sure to please

If Sagittarius is feeling like a nice, relaxing evening—interesting, pleasant, and not *over*-intellectual—the best thing to do is contact a Libran friend, who will be delighted that Sagittarius proposes to come round, and will have plenty of home comforts to offer. Sagittarius can then tell all that's happened since the last time they met, and Libra will listen encouragingly, sympathetically, and advise on Sagittarius' current problems. If Sagittarius feels that Libra ought to be taking a more energetic interest in life, it won't be too difficult to infect Libra with Sagittarian enthusiasm. If Sagittarius suspects that Libra is wasting talent or potential, a simple "Why don't you learn to play that guitar *properly* instead of just strumming away on it?" and Libra should get round to fixing up a series of lessons! So keep it up, Sag! Encouragement and praise will persuade Libra that life is far more worth while than it was before you came on the scene.

When a Sagittarian man is attracted to a Libran lass he'll have found a *very* romantic lady. She loves *love*! She'll fall in love with the emotion rather than the man. She'll be very kind, sweet, attractive—but she'll certainly keep him on a string, for she's as indecisive about her sex life as she is about everything else, putting off decisions as long as possible. Sagittarius may be willing to go along with this for a while—but could then get bored. However, once Libra *does* decide to have a love affair, her chosen man will have a lot of fun in a good deal of comfort. Tact will be needed if the Sagittarian has any other girls in tow at the time, for Libra can be resentful. By finding out where Venus was when she was born (see page 54), he can learn a lot more about her.

When a Sagittarian girl finds a Libran man she should discard jeans and sweater and find some soft, silky number to wear when she plans to catch his eye. He'll be romantic rather than wildly passionate, and will take the pace of the affair from her. But don't let it gallop along, for he's a bit on the languid side and likes to ease gradually into emotional relationships. She'll have rivals, for his charm will have attracted other girls; but then she'll have other boyfriends, too. Like her Sagittarian brothers, she must be tactful about his other friends, for Libra can be prone to jealousy, especially if Venus was in Scorpio at birth.

Basically, Sagittarius and Libra are good together, so there shouldn't be too many problems for them in marriage. Sagittarians can become terribly involved in whatever they are doing and sometimes chaos can result in the home, for Libra's not really in favor of dish-washing!

You and Scorpio

It is difficult to assess whether it's Sagittarius or Scorpio who loves life most. Both are very strong types, and, unsurprisingly, identify with many of the same notions. But they're very different, too. Scorpio is deeply emotional in a smoulderingly intense way. Sagittarius has fiery, enthusiastic emotions that drive them into action. Scorpio will shut up and say nothing; Sagittarius will spill the beans—sometimes rather tactlessly. But it seems likely that the two Signs will meet over some joint project. If they don't a mutual interest will soon develop, for it would be a waste of energy, potential and dyanamic force if something positive failed to emerge from their joint emotion and energy. What? Well, there's plenty of scope: perhaps involvement in a crusade for social justice—the publication of a student or underground magazine, or showing up some failure in the community. Everyone will be the better informed for it, and a lot of people's lives could be made easier as a result of their efforts. Other more overt forms of social work—helping drug addicts, perhaps—could also be done by Sagittarian/Scorpio friends.

When a Sagittarian man is attracted to a well-built Scorpionic brunette (looking exactly as if she's just stepped out of the cast of

Carmen), let him set out to seduce her right away! More than likely, he'll become her lover-boy anyway—but sparks will fly when lively, fun-loving Sagittarius takes another girl out to lunch, for Scorpio can be jealous. He'll do well to find out what Sign Mars was in when she was born (see page 54). Mars is one of her ruling planets and could either heighten or cool her passion. Best for him if it's in Leo, or perhaps Gemini.

A Sagittarian girl attracted to a Scorpio man will find that a lot depends on how dishy she really finds him. If she wants to be swept off her feet, she could certainly arrange it, for he's probably incredibly sexy and passionate. (If she ever feels like playing the uncharacteristic role of heavy seductress, now will be her chance!) He'll be a jealous type which she isn't—so this could just be a short, sharp affair that will broaden her experience of men.

Scorpionic jealousy could tend to mar a Scorpio/Sagittarian marriage—and this won't be helped by Sagittarius' need for freedom of expression. But if both Sagittarius and Scorpio will take account of the differences, they should progress magnificently in material and social life and help each other to mature emotionally. Different ideas about bringing up children must be thoroughly discussed: Sagittarius is easy-going, Scorpio is a disciplinarian.

Gifts that are sure to please

21

You and Sagittarius

Broadly speaking, there are two types of Sagittarian—and very often one loathes the other! One type is all study and books; the other, all sport, fast cars and a large collection of girl or boyfriends, none of whom they really care much for. So when Sagittarius and Sagittarius become friends it's usually the case that both belong firmly to one type. What's interesting for the rest of the human race is when the sporty, devil-may-care Sagittarian develops into the more serious and much nicer type, which is mostly likely to happen if a young, sporty Sag and an old professor Sag make a hit. More commonly, of course, there is a middle course with Sagittarius and Sagittarius throwing out lively and amusing challenges to each other, whether it's making a more complicated dress than the last one or writing an article for a trade journal which will have to be followed up by an even more controversial or studious one.

When a Sagittarius colt finds a Sagittarian filly they will look each other straight in the eye and paw the ground. Then the trotting will start, develop into a canter, and more than likely the filly will jump over the hedge into a field where the grass is greener and a more sophisticated stallion has his eye on her! Buf if the Sagittarian colt is wise, he'll realize that she is only teasing; the stallion isn't her type—too exhausting, and nowhere near as much fun. In no time they will be off again, having fun amid the daffodils and under the apple tree. We would intrude if we followed them further. But seriously, two of this Sign getting together should be set for a delightful, light-hearted affair: the natural sympathy between them will blossom, and each will understand the other's approach and go along with it. If either has Venus in Scorpio (see page 54) there could be a little jealousy, but apart from this they should enjoy a pleasant episode.

A similar partnership of Sagittarian girl and Sagittarian man will be smooth if she is as natural as possible. Sagittarians are unaffected types and blossom when their usually uncomplicated personalities are allowed full freedom of expression. Neither will cramp the other's style—doing their own thing will be a matter of principle for them—and there will be plenty of give and take.

Sagittarius marrying Sagittarius will not need to bother about buying furniture: they will be able to make it out of books, sup-

Gifts that are sure to please

ported here and there by the odd tennis racket and pair of skis!
With luck one might be given an old armchair to sit on; but there
are so many other things more important in life (in Sagittarius'
view) than comfort in the home.

You and Capricorn

Gifts that are sure to please

Jupiter and Saturn—the "gas giants" of the universe—rule Sagittarius and Capricorn respectively. They are opposites in the effect they have on their subjects, as becomes very apparent when Sagittarius and Capricorn are friends. It will be amusing for the rest of their circle to see how they differ yet how they complement each other. If both are psychologically well-developed and have experience of life and people, tolerance, interest in human nature and common sense will prevail. Sagittarius will progress in leaps and bounds, while Capricorn is a steady plodder. So they will argue and discuss their very different outlooks, and of course learn a lot from each other. Sometimes Sagittarius will feel like shooting a few arrows into Capricorn to get him or her moving a little quicker . . . and all too often Capricorn will fear and tremble at Sagittarian risk-taking and sheer foolhardiness. But they will be good for each other.

When a lively Sagittarian man sees his Capricorn girl (probably dressed in dark grey or black) he could be put off by her cool, unemotional manner—so different from his own. But let him get to know her, for she can be very lively and great fun to be with. She's marvelous to tease (when she knows the man who's teasing), for she has a great sense of humor. She's ambitious and may be rather formal, so Sagittarian man should put on his best Sunday suit when he takes her on a date. She'll probably be musical, and will appreciate being asked to a concert.

When a Sagittarian girl spots a city-suited Capricornian man it's not much good her saying, "Hi!—let's go for a beer at lunch-time." She'll have to be much more formal, perhaps giving a dinner party for him and a few other friends. (She mustn't ask him to her place alone; even if he's young and stylish, he'll think that not exactly correct.) He could be a bit aloof, but a glass or two of the best wine from Daddy's cellar should help warm his chilly heart. He will probably be ambitious and want to get on in the world, so if she can name-drop, or casually mention that her uncle is chairman of such-and-such a company, his ears will prick up. She must remember he could well be far less emotional than she.

When Sagittarius marries Capricorn, one must try to steady the other, blending the many very opposite characteristics mentioned above. They could then do very well, for Sagittarian ideas and broad vision plus Capricornian care could move mountains. Sagittarian's informality of life-style versus Capricorn's liking for strict formality could cause some difficulties.

You and Aquarius

When Sagittarius and Aquarius become friends they should be very stimulated by each other's opinions, outlook and attitude to life. They will love going out together—to anything from an archaeological dig to a cook-out on some beach on Midsummer night. Intellectually speaking, while Sagittarius is able to shoot arrows off at a fairly fast and furious rate, and indeed over some distance, Aquarius goes even faster and farther; so great mental journeys will be taken together. Inspiration, imagination and perhaps a great deal of scientific thinking can all come together in a Sagittarian/Aquarian friendship—right from childhood, when kids of these Signs at school together will make up fantastic stories to delight each other, to teenagers embroidering their adventures and, in later life, men and women with a fine sense of vision, inspiration and intellect join forces. While the Sagittarian mind is more traditional than the Aquarian, which is

Gifts that are sure to please

very advanced and unconventional, they can make a dynamic combination.

When a warm Sagittarian man is attracted to a friendly but distant Aquarian winter lovely he'll certainly hear icicles tinkling instead of bells ringing. She'll be very friendly and very, very kind; but emotionally she'll be miles away. He will respect her need for freedom and her love of independence, for this will mirror his own. If he can melt her heart—and he should be in a good position to do so—he will have a lovely, faithful girlfriend who won't mind about his other loves. He should find out when she was born, and look up the position of Venus at the time (see page 54). His life will be a lot easier if it was in Sagittarius. If it was in Capricorn or Aquarius, she will *really* be a cool customer, and the ice will be that much thicker!

When a Sagittarian girl finds her film-star Aquarian man she, too, will have to get busy with the ice pick. But she'll find that he'll be extremely friendly, and will be delighted to be asked out for a lunchtime drink. He's usually pretty forward-looking, but he can be stubborn once he has made up his mind about issues, so there's something of an intellectual challenge about him, too. The real challenge will of course come from the emotional point of view, and she could well learn quickly that he could respond to her sexually, but may think of sex as a necessity rather than a pleasure.

When Sagittarius marries Aquarius they will no doubt both continue to do their own things, for Sagittarius is freedom-loving and freedom-needing, and Aquarius is equally independent. All well and good—but be careful!

You and Pisces

From time immemorial until 1846, Jupiter ruled both Sagittarius and Pisces. Now, while most modern astrologers bear in mind that Jupiter has a hand in the affairs of Pisces, they think primarily in terms of Neptune, who came on the scene in Victorian times and gradually assumed more and more importance. Not difficult, then, to see that there is a natural sympathy between these Signs (not unlike the relationship between Taurus and Libra, the Venusian Signs). Of the two, Sagittarius is definitely the stronger and more philosophical; Pisces is more inspired, and often more religious. The Sagittarian will either very strongly accept religious convictions or as strongly reject them; Pisces is attracted not so much by dogma as by the inspirational, spiritual aspects. When a Sagittarian and a Piscean become friends, emotions of this kind can unite them on a level which may not require discussion—they will simply feel right together. In a more mundane way they will have some enjoyable times, but Sagittarius may have to work hard on Pisces, helping to encourage a not always fully expressed creative potential.

When Sagittarius the philosopher meets Pisces the poetess, he can be his natural self and talk to her in a quiet corner: joint interests will soon emerge. He must remember that she will have a very high emotional level, which is in itself rather complex. It's not *his* kind of emotion at all. She could get involved too easily with men, and has probably been hurt already, even if she's quite young. So he ought to try to steady her emotionally, holding back a little to give her time to get him in perspective.

When the Sagittarian girl, glancing up from her books in the library, sees a delicious man eyeing her from behind a pile of poetry books, they will both soon be off on a trip to paradise. This affair should be memorable and happy, though there are sure to be times when their very different emotions clash. Pisces may not take too easily to the brighter, more extroverted, freedom-loving side of Sagittarius, so she'll have to be careful if she accepts a date with someone else.

When Sagittarius and Pisces marry it seems likely that the easy-going side of both will help them to develop plenty of give and take, which will certainly be of help. It will most likely be a highly-spiced and emotional marriage, with terrific ups and downs. But there will also be a lot of fun, for both have a good sense of humor which they will enjoy sharing.

Gifts that are sure to please

Making the most of Sagittarius

Jupiter, the ruling planet of Sagittarius, has a dignified influence over the colors of the Sign, for here we have regal purple and deep blue predominating. Most Sagittarians look terrific in these colors. If they do not usually wear purple, they should consider it: it really can do something for them, in an almost uncanny way.

Most Sagittarians are not over-conscious of their image. There is very often something of the eternal student about them—they have their minds mostly on other things, and may sometimes think their image unimportant. They are usually delightful, enthusiastic people, with broad, intelligent foreheads and their lively, responsive, quick-changing expressions are part of their enormously open personalities. While they would never consciously use this as part of their image, it naturally comes through, so from this point of view Sagittarians quite unconsciously make the most of themselves.

The girls, like the men, look fine in casual clothes—shirts, slacks and jeans. Polo-necked sweaters are marvelous for them, and so are fur-lined anoraks. But for a real touch of drama, they might like to try a long, flowing cloak, perhaps in purple, and let the Jupiter influence really take over! They love the open *air* and the rarefied atmosphere of the college library and dress accordingly. We see them looking fantastic in country clothes, or dressed for comfort rather than style when poring over books.

There's no doubt about it—the Sagittarian girl needs a very large handbag indeed! A portmanteau or hold-all would be a better way to describe it. She will always be loaded down to the ground with books, papers, sports gear—all manner of things —and will do well to search out the biggest bag in town. Besides, she'll *like* something very large, for she is not usually small in build and she can look good with something queen-sized! She'll like to wear healthy, open-cut sandals and comfortable shoes, which suit her life-style; to her, this will be much more important than her image, or the way she *should* look. The choice of tights will be a source of fun and variety for the Sagittarian girl, who could well experiment quite a lot with these, turning up every day in something new and different. She may like fine, interesting and really lacy tights for more formal occasions, and vivid, striped "football sock" designs for day-to-day wear!

Unfortunately for Sagittarius, the metal of the Sign is humble tin! Still, one can find some fashionable and amusing pendants and necklaces in this metal, which are fun to wear. The gem is a splended one: the topaz—and if she can get a Spanish topaz (for Spain is a Sagittarian country), Jupiter can be proud of her indeed!

The men cling rather more than the girls, perhaps, to the student image, and while no one would want to change a Sagittarian (they are far too interesting and pleasant for that), they can do a very great deal for themselves just by developing their sense of style. Sagittarian males usually hate ties, for instance. Well, that's fine, provided they add a dashing scarf (perhaps in a rich

yellow) to the open collar of their shirt. They are among the few people who can get away with this when wearing a formal suit, and look splendid—casual enough to look sexy, but not enough to upset anybody.

All Sagittarians need physical exercise far more than any other sign of the Zodiac, and they should have some spare-time interest that is physically demanding. The girls might like to take a fairly strenuous modern dance class, if they are not already engaged in some sport. The men need a similar outlet—perhaps a work-out in a gym, as Sagittarians tend to put on weight quite easily if over-absorbed in intellectual pursuits.

The Sagittarian pad will be a place full of interest—and books. One may well have to move a pile of them before relaxing on what will probably be the oldest settee in the world. But Sagittarius is very aware of the opposite sex, and will make sure that in spite of the books there will be an area where they can practice the gentle art of seduction in an atmosphere that is just right for them.

The Astrology of Love

Astrology at work

"The celestial bodies are the cause of all that takes place in the sub-lunar world"

Thomas Aquinas

Astrology must have started, in ages so remote from our own that all trace of them has vanished, by man noticing the simplest facts: that the Moon affected the tides, and made fishing easier or more difficult; that when Mars showed his red face in certain areas of the sky, a tribe fought more fiercely. . . . Then, in clear Eastern skies, the seven planets known to ancient man were observed to make a pattern in the heavens—a pattern that meant something.

It was when a well-organized priesthood grew up in Babylonia that man really began to study the planets' effects on human life—at first very simply, noting only the moments when planets rose and set—but then observing, too, the effects of planets at certain angles to other planets. Written notes of planetary movements exist from 747 B.C., so astrology has a *written* history of over 2,700 years.

The solar system, *with the Sun at its center. Copernicus, in 1548, put forward the theory that the Sun, rather than Earth, was at the center of the system. The general theory of astrology was not affected by this, as Isaac Newton, who developed it, knew.*

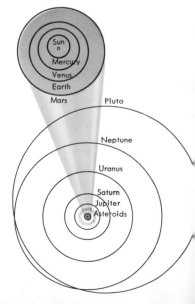

For many centuries, from the earliest years of astrology, men believed that the planets' effect was supernatural. At first they were associated with the gods, and later it was still believed that their action was in some way spiritual. But modern astrologers look at it another way.

It is now more often believed that the positions of the planets at any one moment in time have an effect on earth through some force like, but not the same as, that of gravity. Science tells us that during the first half-hour after conception many human traits, physical and psychological, are formed within the tiny egg that is to become a man or woman. It may be at that time that the planets (known to affect vegetable and plant growth and the behavior of animals) also affect the human egg and the subsequent life of the child — among other things, his or her human capacity for affection, friendship and love.

Scientists rather than astrologers must discover precisely "how astrology works." At the moment we know nothing about the kind of force that can cross the vast reaches of space between Pluto and Earth and have an effect on human life. But compared with the unimaginable distances of outer space, the solar system is a small and compact unit, not unlike an atomic nucleus. In a sense, it would be extraordinary if the planets that nestle around the Sun did not affect us on Earth. As J. S. Haldane put it: 'The universe may be not only queerer than we suppose, but queerer than we *can* suppose!'

The birth chart

The complete Birth Chart is a map of the sky for the moment and from the place of birth

Page 37 is a complete Birth Chart, used by an astrologer to discover the true potentialities of a client—his or her strong and weak points, the most suitable career and, of course, where he or she might expect to find most happiness in love. Earth is the center of the Chart. Around it, the twelve equal Signs of the Zodiac form a band against which the planets move. The astrologer has placed them precisely as they were at the moment when his client was born. Everyone has *all* the planets and *all* the Signs in his or her Birth Chart. By looking at their positions—in relation to the Earth and to each other, in the twelve Signs, and in the "houses" (the twelve inner segments of the Chart)—the astrologer begins to interpret the effect they have on the client's personality. The Sign the Sun occupies (in this case, Gemini) is important; but so too is the Ascendant (Pisces), the Midheaven (Sagittarius), the Sign the Moon is in (Pisces), and all the rest.

To discover trends in their clients' future lives (astrologers never "foretell the future"; the planets cannot dictate what *will* happen, they can only suggest what may happen), astrologers "progress" the Birth Chart. Having calculated the precise position of every planet at the moment of birth, they use one of several methods to "move" them to new positions that symbolize possible future pleasures or hazards: when, for instance, you might expect a romance or even marriage.

Each planet "rules" a Sign, which means that it is stronger when placed in that Sign at birth. It also has a special relationship with other planets, according to the Signs they are in. The planets (inner circle) are shown "in" the Signs they traditionally rule.

Glyphs of the Signs		Glyphs of the Planets	
♈ Aries	♎ Libra	☉ Sun	♄ Saturn
♉ Taurus	♏ Scorpio	☽ Moon	♅ Uranus
♊ Gemini	♐ Sagittarius	☿ Mercury	♆ Neptune
♋ Cancer	♑ Capricorn	♀ Venus	♇ Pluto
♌ Leo	♒ Aquarius	♂ Mars	☊ Moon's Nodes: North
♍ Virgo	♓ Pisces	♃ Jupiter	☋ South

Ascendant or Rising Sign
The sign rising on the eastern horizon at the moment of birth: here shown as 24° Pisces: once the position of the Ascendant is calculated, the other signs follow in order round the Chart.

Cusp of First House
The inner circle of the Chart is divided into 12 equal Houses: the First House occupies the 30° area below the eastern horizon; the cusp marks its starting-point.

Moon's Nodes
The nodes are the north and south points at which the Moon crosses the ecliptic: the north node is shown here in Pisces, the south node is at the opposite point in Virgo.

Glyphs of Planets
The glyphs of the planets (Saturn is the example marked here) are placed round the Chart and their exact positions at the moment of birth are noted in figures.

MC or Medium Coeli
The MC (Midheaven) is the point at which the ecliptic crosses the subject's meridian; in general terms the MC is the overhead point in the sky.

Glyphs of Signs
The sign glyphs, like that of Scorpio indicated here, are inserted round the Chart once the Ascendant is calculated. The glyphs are an extremely ancient form of shorthand.

Descendant
The opposite end of the Horizon line to the Ascendant; i.e. the degree of the Zodiac setting beneath the western horizon, here shown as 24° Virgo.

Aspect Lines
Aspect lines on the Chart draw attention to specific angular relationships between planets, as seen from Earth. Aspects are of the utmost importance in interpretation.

Line of Horizon
This line divides the Birth Chart in two: planets appear either above the horizon (upper half of Chart) or below it. Here the Sun's position denotes a birth-time after midnight.

IC or Imum Coeli
This is the opposite point on the Chart to the MC or Medium Coeli, i.e. the point in the sky more or less beneath the subject's feet at the moment of his birth.

Cusp of Sign
The cusp of a sign marks the starting-point of a new sign; a planet appearing precisely on the cusp in our illustration would be placed on 0° Gemini (not 30° Taurus).

House Divisions
The 12 Houses relate to specific areas of the subject's life, e.g. possessions, career, family, etc.; although other forms exist, the Equal House System is used throughout this book.

37

Signs of the Zodiac

How the heavens determine character

Though astrological columns print paragraphs suggesting what the future has in store for "Aries" or "Gemini", this can be only very roughly true. For you—and what may happen to you in the future—are a mixture of all the influences of all the Signs, more or less stressed by the position of the planets within them. Though if you were born at or near sunrise, you may find that the news for "Gemini", or the character-analysis of "your" Sign printed in a magazine or newspaper, is more accurate than for other people. This is because the Sun Sign in your Birth Chart will be the same as the Ascendant. But even then, the full Birth Chart should be calculated before you can really be sure that you know the whole truth about your astrological self.

Your Sun Sign—and you will certainly know what *that* is, because it depends on the time of year you were born; it is what people mean when they say "I am a Leo" or "an Aries"—generally shows the image you present to the world. The Ascendant, which you can only discover by having it calculated, represents your inner, "true" self. You may behave or look very like a Leo, but if your Ascendant is, say, Sagittarius, then your real inner self will be very different from your outward appearance.

A professional astrologer will go much further, considering not only planetary positions but also the angles between the planets, the relevant "polarities"—triplicities and quadruplicities. Polarities link the qualities of the Signs in an interesting and strong way. Aries people, for instance, may tend to be somewhat self-centered; Librans (Libra is the opposite Sign to Aries across the Zodiac) tend to be strongly geared to "the other person."

The Quadruplicities again group Signs of the Zodiac together and give them certain qualities. People with an emphasis on Cardinal Signs (Aries, Cancer, Libra, Capricorn) tend to be enterprising and outgoing. An emphasis on Fixed Signs (Taurus, Leo, Scorpio, Aquarius) prompts resistance to change. Those with many planets in the Mutable Signs (Gemini, Virgo, Sagittarius, Pisces) tend to be adaptable and subject to change.

The qualities that the Quadruplicities show must be considered in relation to the Triplicities, and also, as always, to the appearance of the whole Birth Chart.

The Keywords are a shorthand way of remembering very roughly the qualities of each Zodiac Sign: they represent the way in which each Sign expresses itself. The keywords for Aries are "assertively, urgently." For Taurus: "possessively, permanently." Gemini: "communicatively, adaptably." Cancer: "protectively, sensitively." Leo: "creatively, impressively, powerfully." Virgo: "critically, analytically." Libra: "harmoniously, together." Scorpio: "intensively, passionately." Sagittarius: "widely, freely, exploratively." Capricorn: "prudently, aspiringly, calculatedly." Aquarius: "independently, humanely." Pisces: "nebulously, impressionably."

The Triplicities
Zodiac Signs are divided into Fire Signs, Earth Signs, Air Signs and Water Signs—astrologers find that when, for instance, Water Signs are emphasized by the planets in them at the time of birth, the subject has some of the qualities of the "watery" Signs.

Fire *Signs contribute enthusiasm.*

Earth *Signs: stability and practicality.*

Air *Signs: intellectualism, ease of communication.*

Water *Signs: emotion and intuition.*

# Synastry

Charting the chances of love

This whole book is about what astrologers call "synastry"—in its simplest form. When two clients ask an astrologer just how well they might get on in love or marriage, it won't be possible to tell them simply from their Sun Signs. Even the positions of Mars and Venus in their Birth Charts won't decide the matter.

The astrologer will draw up both their Birth Charts, complete, showing all the planets in all the Signs, and the two Charts will be compared with great care before anything at all is said. And even then, the astrologer will be very careful indeed. What he or she will do is point out the areas of their lives in which they are likely to find agreement and happiness, and those other areas where there might be some difficulty.

Julia Parker, a consultant astrologer, has worked on many pairs of Charts on this basis, and has tried to do the same in this book. That is, she has tried to hint fairly strongly at the similarities and differences between the Sun Sign characteristics, and has sometimes suggested that the positions of Venus and Mars (pages 54 and 60) may be helpful. But of course it would be silly to drop a new friend because "the stars" don't seem to be on the side of friendship. There may be other factors in the complete Birth Charts which promise well.

The serious astrologer uses synastry—the comparison of Birth Charts—in many ways: not only when marriage is a possibility, but when there is perhaps a prospect of a marriage breaking up. The astrologer will then compare not two but three Charts —those for Mr A and Mrs A and X, the other man or woman in the case. By "progressing" the Charts, it is almost always possible to tell, for instance, if the extra-marital affair is one that is going to last or is just a passing infatuation.

Synastry can explore business partnerships or look at the parent/child relationship. It can also be used in the teacher/student situation, and in many others. One thing is very important—in all aspects of astrology, but perhaps more so in synastry. That is that the full birth data must be available. Sometimes a boy will bring his own birth date, time and place, but only the girl's birth date. This means that the astrologer will not be able to work out the Ascendant, or the Sign on the Midheaven (see page 37), and factors will be missing from the assessment.

Critics have accused astrologers of trying to "run people's lives." But the destiny of friends and lovers is in their own hands. The planets can help or hinder—but can be overruled.

Tina and Tony were engaged. They knew their Sun Signs—Tina was Taurus, Tony was Aries—and they were worried when they found a book that said, "Aries and Taurus rarely get on together, and marriage would be unwise." Unhappy, they went to consult an astrologer.

She was a reputable astrologer. "That's nonsense," she said, "a huge over-simplification. What really matters is the story of your Birth Charts as a whole."

She drew up complete Birth Charts for them both. "Popular astrologers are so unreliable," she said to herself. "It's quite clear, from their Charts, that Tina and Tony will get on very well in marriage."

Tina and Tony were thrilled when the astrologer told them. "Naturally, there are certain areas where you can expect to disagree," her report warned. "But I have no doubt that, if you play down your differences, you will both be very happy." And, you know, they were.

Planets of love

"Astrology is astronomy brought to earth and applied to the affairs of men" —

Emerson

In this book we can deal only with the Sun Sign—the Zodiac Sign in which the Sun was placed at the moment of birth—and the positions of Venus and Mars (see pages 54-64). An astrologer advising anyone about their love life, or perhaps the end of an affair, would rely on a full Birth Chart (see page 37). For of course it is not only the position of the Sun which has an effect on one's love life, but *all* the planets in *all* the Signs.

The Sun. This book is largely based on the effect the Sun has on love when it is in various Signs.

Venus is associated with the desire for lasting partnership. It can make one over-gushing, over-romantic—but the positions of other planets will affect this. For the position of Venus in your own Chart, consult pages 54—59.

Mars. If Venus is a feminine and romantic planet, Mars is masculine and sensual. It can make one rather selfish and hasty—but see pages 60—64 for its position in your Chart.

The Moon can be responsible for emotional disturbance. It can make one patient and sympathetic—and also changeable and narrow-minded. It moves very quickly and its position must be carefully calculated.

Mercury affects communication with other people, affecting the way you talk to them and put over your feelings. It will either be in the same Sign as your Sun, or the one on either side. If you are Aries, for example, your Mercury will either be in Aries, Pisces or Taurus.

Jupiter. In Holst's Suite *The Planets*, Jupiter is called "the Bringer of Jollity", and can indeed contribute generosity, enjoyment, sheer *fun* to an affair, particularly if you happen to meet a partner whose Jupiter is in the same Sun as your own. This planet stays in each Sign for a year.

Saturn. That icy planet, Saturn, can really cool down an affair, for it can make one cautious, thrifty, selfish—break things up in no time at all!

Uranus can make one versatile and original, but it can also contribute eccentricity and even perversion. But at work in two Charts it can also mean a sudden dynamic attraction.

Neptune. Those with Neptune strong in their Chart will be idealistic, sensitive, spiritual—or could be deceitful, sentimental and indecisive, depending on the rest of the Birth Chart. But the planet can certainly bring romance! Those born between 1915-1928/9 will have Neptune in Leo; between 1928/9-1942/3 in Virgo; between 1942/3-1956/7 in Libra. If Neptune is in Leo, it can contribute glamour and perhaps self-satisfaction; if in Virgo, an over-critical attitude; if in Libra, unworldly idealism and perhaps an attraction to drugs.

Pluto affects the beginnings or endings of affairs—the ability to make a new start, perhaps under difficult conditions. From 1913/14-1937/8 Pluto was in Cancer; from 1937/8-1957 in Leo; from 1958/9-1971 in Virgo. Pluto in Cancer involved its generation in sudden changes in family life—often the disruption suffered during wartime. In Leo, Pluto seems to be prompting increased interest in mass social security and love for the whole family of nations and its environment. In Virgo, it could lead to a total re-evaluation of personal relationships, love and the family.

But how do astrologers know when romance is about to blossom for us? Modern astrologers do not predict events, but can discover periods when an emotional relationship may deepen, though not when one *will* get married. As one gets older, one's Birth Chart grows older too, and the planets in the Chart make new relationships to each other, which themselves in time break up, more forming in their place. When, for instance, Venus and the Sun come together or Venus and romantic Neptune shake hands, there is a powerful emphasis on the love life. As in every other area of life, what matters is not the Sun Sign alone but the whole Chart.

But do the planets then *compel* two people to love or not to love each other? Of course not. Even a couple with dreadfully clashing Charts would have a chance together, for, as the old astrological motto says, "The stars *incline*, they do not compel." Man (and woman) is still the master of Fate. Certainly, when you are thinking of that first date, it can do no harm at all to find out where his Mars is, or where her Venus. But if you are attracted to each other—go ahead. The most the planets can ever say is, "We told you so!" They will never claim that they made the match.

Astrology and the body

In earlier centuries a doctor was almost invariably also an astrologer—in fact, one was not allowed to study medicine unless one also studied planetary effects on the human body, in sickness and health.

The various parts of the body were traditionally influenced by certain Signs, and the planets themselves were associated with specific illnesses, and more recently with the glandular system—particularly the endocrine glands that release hormones into the blood. The Sun, for instance, which traditionally rules the heart, back and spinal column, is now associated with the thymus as well. The Moon is associated with the breasts and the digestive system. Venus, always known to affect the throat and kidneys, is now also connected with the parathyroids. And Mars, associated through the ages with the sexual impulse, acts also on the urogenital system and gonads. Saturn is associated with the skin.

Just as the traditional connections between the Signs and parts of the body can be used in medicine, so too can they be used in love-making to ensure a happier and more fulfilled partnership.

Very little real study has been given to this area of astrology: it is fun, and contributes to a happy love-relationship to note how a loved one reacts to the sense of touch in connection with the Birth Chart. Here is a rough check-list of Signs and their associated parts of the body. The polarities—opposite Signs—often react the same, which is why they are paired.

Gemini/Sagittarius: arms, shoulders
Leo/Aquarius: spine and back
Libra/Aries: kidneys
Scorpio/Taurus: sexual organs
Capricorn/Cancer: knees and teeth
Pisces/Virgo: feet
Aries/Libra: head
Taurus/Scorpio: throat and neck
Cancer/Capricorn: stomach, breasts
Virgo/Pisces: nervous system
Sagittarius/Gemini: hips and thighs
Aquarius/Leo: shins, ankles, veins

The herbs of love

Seasoning the food of love

From time immemorial, man has used herbs as medicines. And the men and women of Shakespeare's age used herbs in love—as aphrodisiacs, to beautify the body and to encourage sexual health. The most thorough study of herbs and their uses was made by the 17th century astrologer-physician Nicholas Culpeper, whose *Herbal*, published in the 1640s, is still in print.

Culpeper associated all herbs with their ruling planets and suggested that "such as are astrologers (and indeed none else are fit to make physicians)" should gather the herbs when the planet governing them was rising, setting, or immediately overhead, and with the Moon "in good aspect." He also gives careful instructions for their use; and today anyone experimenting in the use of herbs as medicine should take the precaution of consulting an acknowledged herbalist before preparing and taking potions, some of which may be poisonous.

Culpeper, though he pointed out some herbs which "stir up venery or bodily lust," kept carefully away from the whole question of aphrodisiacs—which indeed remain controversial and dangerous. Powders prepared from the insect cantharides (the notorious "Spanish Fly") can cause serious damage to the gastro-intestinal system, which it inflames; yohimbine, from the bark of the African yohimbé tree, can cripple.

There are more innocent aphrodisiacs, though whether they work or not is questionable. The sweet potato, chestnuts, onions, eringo and asparagus are all pleasant to eat, whether or not they have any effect in the courts of love. Carrots, now served at almost every dinner, were in Elizabethan days said to be "great furtherers of Venus her pleasure and of love's delights"! None of these, we suppose, are very likely to harm; and perhaps equally unlikely to help.

Miscellany of Love

Putting emotions into words

One of the pleasures, you might even say one of the duties, of being in love is to *celebrate* the fact. And it's not difficult. When you're in love, bells are ringing, the skies seem always blue, the stars are always shining, moon rhymes with June, and just to be alive is celebration enough. . . .

On the other hand, not many lovers are particularly good at expressing their feelings, and shared experience often has to be a substitute for the joy a painter might put into a picture, a composer into a serenade, a poet into a poem. We see a film together, and the love story on the screen becomes part of our love story; we hear a tune, and ever after it is 'our tune'; we read a poem, and its lines say exactly what we would say, if we could find the words.

Poets strive to describe what, for the rest of us, is indescribable. The emotion of love is one of the most difficult things in the world to express in anything other than a look or a gesture, so it is not surprising that most poets have, at some time, written love poetry. Here are a few lines from some of the world's greatest love poetry. Read them—alone or together. They will not only enrich your own experience, they will perhaps open the door a little on the whole idea of love—what it means to love tenderly, passionately, hopelessly. Through them, you can share the joy of other men and women, making your own experience part of a *world* of lovers.

We love being in love, that's the truth on't.
　　　　　　—W. M. THACKERAY

Love goes toward love, as schoolboys from their books;
But love from love, toward school with heavy looks.
　　　　　　—WILLIAM SHAKESPEARE

Love is the wisdom of the fool and the folly
of the wise.
　　　　　　—SAMUEL JOHNSON

Youth's the season made for joys,
Love is then our duty.
　　　　　　—JOHN GAY

Rosaline

Like to the clear in highest sphere
 Where all imperial glory shines,
Of self-same colour is her hair
 Whether unfolded or in twines
  Heigh ho, fair Rosaline!
Her eyes are sapphires set in snow,
 Resembling heaven by every wink;
The gods do fear when as they glow
 And I do tremble when I think
  Heigh ho, would she were mine!

Her cheeks are like the blushing cloud
 That beautifies Aurora's face,
Or like the silver crimson shroud
 That Phoebus' smiling looks doth grace:
  Heigh ho, fair Rosaline!
Her lips are like two budded roses
 Whom ranks of lilies neighbour nigh,
Within whose bounds she balm encloses
 Apt to entice a deity:
  Heigh ho, would she were mine!

—THOMAS LODGE

No Limits

*I cannot exist without you. I am forgetful
of everything but seeing you again—my
life seems to stop there—I see no further.
You have absorbed me. I have a sensation
at the present moment as though I was
dissolving—I should be exquisitely
miserable without the hope of soon
seeing you. I should be afraid to separate
myself far from you. . . . I have no limit
not to my love. Love is my religion.
I could die for that. I could die for you.*

—JOHN KEATS

*Diaphenia, like the daffadowndilly,
White as the sun, fair as the lily,
Heigh ho, how I do love thee!*

—HENRY CHETTLE

*But to see her was to love her,
Love but her, and love for ever.*

—ROBERT BURNS

O Mistress Mine

O mistress mine, where are you roaming?
O stay and hear, your true love's coming
   That can sing both high and low.
Trip no further, pretty sweeting;
Journeys end in lovers meeting,
   Every wise man's son doth know.

What is love? 'Tis not hereafter:
Present mirth hath present laughter,
   What's to come is still unsure.
In delay there lies no plenty—
Then come kiss me, sweet-and-twenty:
   Youth's a stuff will not endure.

          —WILLIAM SHAKESPEARE

Next to being married, a girl likes to
be crossed in love a little now and then.
         —JANE AUSTEN

Love in Thy Youth

Love in thy youth, fair maid; be wise,
   Old time will make thee colder,
And though each morning new arise
   Yet we each day grow older.

Thou as heaven art fair and young,
   Thine eyes like twin stars shining:
But ere another day be sprung
   All these will be declining.

Then winter comes with all his fears
   And all thy sweets shall borrow;
Too late then wilt thou shower thy tears,
   And I too late shall sorrow.

          —ANON.

Love sought is good, but given unsought is
better.
         —WILLIAM SHAKESPEARE

Sweet, Let Me Go

Sweet, let me go! sweet, let me go!
What do you mean to vex me so?
Cease your pleading force!
Do you think thus to extort
   remorse?
Now, now, no more! alas; you
   overbear me,
And I would cry,
—but some would hear, I fear me.

—ANON.

How Do I Love Thee?

How do I love thee? Let me count the ways.
I love thee to the depth and breadth and height
My soul can reach, when feeling out of sight
For the ends of Being and ideal Grace.
I love thee to the level of every day's
Most quiet need, by sun and candle-light..
I love thee freely, as men strive for right;
I love thee purely, as they turn from praise.
I love thee with the passion put to use
In my old griefs, and with my childhood's faith.
I love thee with a love I seemed to lose
With my lost saints—I love thee with the breath,
Smiles, tears, of all my life!—and, if God choose,
I shall but love thee better after death.

—ELIZABETH BARRETT BROWNING

Remember

Remember me when I am gone away,
Gone far away into the silent land;
When you can no more hold me by the hand,
Nor I half turn to go yet turning stay.
Remember me when no more day by day
You tell me of our future that you planned;
Only remember me; you understand
It will be late to counsel then or pray.
Yet if you should forget me for a while
And afterwards remember, do not grieve:
For if the darkness and corruption leave
A vestige of the thoughts that once I had,
Better by far you should forget and smile
Than that you should remember and be sad.

—CHRISTINA ROSSETTI

Love rules the court, the camp, the grove,
And men below, and saints above;
For love is heaven, and heaven is love.

—SIR WALTER SCOTT

The Kiss

O that joy so soon should waste!
  Or so sweet a bliss
  As a kiss
Might not for ever last!
So sugared, so melting, so soft,
  so delicious,
  The dew that lies on roses,
  When the moon herself discloses,
Is not so precious.
O, rather than it would I smother,
Were I to taste such another;
  It should be my wishing
  That I might die kissing.

—BEN JONSON

Let's Now Take Our Time

Let's now take our time
While we're in our prime,
And old, old age is afar off:
For the evil, evil days
Will come on apace
Before we can be aware of.

—ROBERT HERRICK

Sleep is still most perfect, in spite of hygienists,
when it is shared with a beloved. The warmth, the
security and peace of soul, the utter comfort from
the touch of the other, knits the sleep, so that it
takes the body and soul completely in its healing.

—D. H. LAWRENCE

Where's your Venus?

The emotional side of love

Venus influences the capacity for love and affection, Mars a man's or a woman's sexual response. The effects of Venus are strongest when it is in Taurus or Libra. If your Venus is in the same Sign as your Sun, what you read about your love life under your Zodiac Sign ought to be accurate; if Venus falls in a different Sign, this gives another dimension to the expression of your love. In order to find out where your own or your partner's Venus is, turn to the astrological tables on page 57—59. First find your year of birth on the top line of the table and then your month of birth at the lefthand side of the chart (1=January, 2=February, etc.). The table shows in which Sign of the Zodiac Venus was on the first of each month and also any date during that month on which it moved to another Sign. For instance, if you look at the table, you will see that in January 1947 Venus was in Scorpio on the first of the month, and moved into Sagittarius on January 6th.

VENUS THROUGH THE SIGNS

Venus in Aries ♈
A warm and affectionate man or woman; probably very emotional, but with fiery, positive emotion. Best summed up as ardent and true—but watch out for selfishness, especially if the Sun Sign is Aries when, although there will be kindness, there may also be self-seeking tendencies.

Venus in Taurus ♉
Here is someone who will lavish affection on a partner, and contribute much to the development of a relationship. Possessiveness is bound to be present, and the loved one will almost inevitably be thought of as "mine," in much the same way as any other treasured possession.

Venus in Gemini ♊
Those who have Venus in this Sign will enjoy their relationships, and perhaps take them rather lightly. There is a strong possibility that they will have "more than one string to their bow," and they can find themselves in love with two people at the same time.

Venus in Cancer ♋

This placing contributes much tenderness and a strong tendency to look after the loved one. A certain claustrophobic feeling may be in evidence, because the person is so cherishing or sentimental. They may also dwell in the past too much. A high emotional level is very likely.

Venus in Leo ♌

Love, affection and loyalty will be expressed in a grand and probably expensive way, especially if the Sun Sign is Leo or Libra. There may be a tendency to dominate or rule the partner, and dramatic scenes are possible!

Venus in Virgo ♍

This tends to contribute over-critical, clinical or chaste tendencies, inhibiting a full, satisfactory expression of love; so conflict can occur, especially if the Sun Sign is loving, romantic Libra. The need for a "perfect" partner may be a root cause of difficulty in relationships.

Venus in Libra ♎ ✓

This placing indicates a whole-hearted romantic who is not a fully integrated person until he or she is enjoying a permanent relationship. If the Sun Sign is Virgo, this will warm the matter-of-fact, practical Virgoan heart. Powerfully romantic and affectionate feelings are inevitable.

Venus in Scorpio ♏

Considerable intensity, emotion and intuition will be very evident in the expression of affection and feelings. Jealousy and possessiveness may mar the relationship, and a very "black-and-white" attitude to love is very likely. These tendencies are modified if the Sun Sign is Libra of Sagittarius.

Venus in Sagittarius ♐

This is definitely a lively position for Venus, and the overall attitude to love and relationships may not be too serious. More than one relationship is likely, and there is also an idealistic facet, which is very positive. Great warmth, affection and enthusiasm will be fully expressed, however.

Venus in Capricorn ♑

Venus's influence in this Sign is chilly, but once the barriers are broken one finds an extremely loyal, faithful, and dependable person. There will be few words of affection, but what is said is meant—especially if the Sun Sign is Capricorn, rather than Sagittarius.

Venus in Aquarius ♒

This placing nearly always contributes a sort of film-star glamour; if the Sun Sign is Capricorn it may be a little difficult to come really close to that person—physically or emotionally, but especially emotionally. There is often a marked tendency towards platonic friendships rather than romantic relationships.

Venus in Pisces ♓

A kind, loving, willing slave who cannot do enough for one! Life could become blissfully romantic in an unorganized way. There should be very little difficulty in getting on with a "Venus in Pisces," though emotions could well run rather high at times.

Venus chart

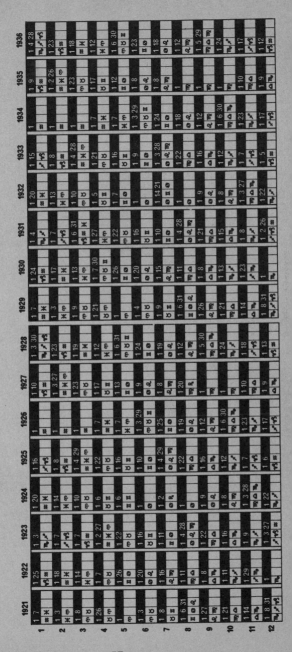

Venus chart

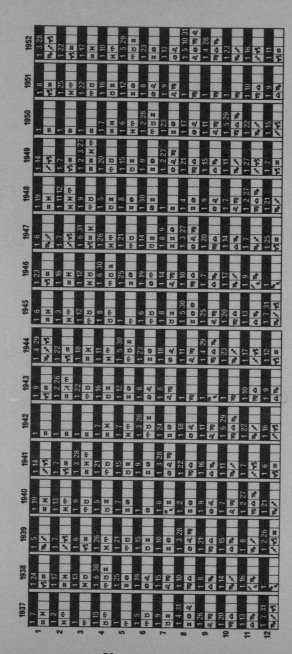

Venus chart

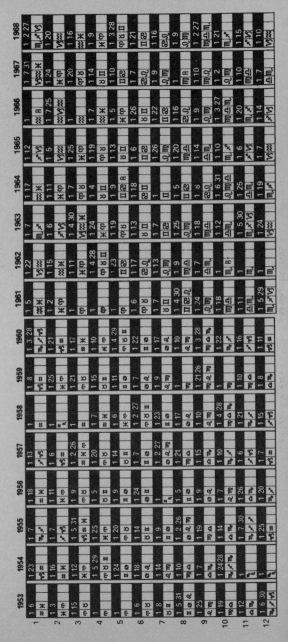

Where's your Mars?

The way love finds expression

Mars is at its strongest in Aries and in Scorpio.

Now turn to the table on pages 62—64 and find out where your Mars (and your partner's!) were on your birth dates. The procedure is exactly the same as it was for finding your Venus, and the table will show you in which Sign Mars was on the first day of any month, and the day or days in that month when it moved to another Sign.

MARS THROUGH THE SIGNS

Mars in Aries ♈
Mars in Aries will contribute highly sexed and passionate tendencies. The person will be demanding, but straightforward and good company. There will be enthusiasm, warmth and energy, and a general feeling that life is to be enjoyed.

Mars in Taurus ♉
An extremely passionate and highly sexed man or woman. Feelings are usually slow to be roused, but once aroused sexual desire is strong. Jealousy and possessiveness can often creep into relationships. People with Mars in Taurus are extremely sensual, sexually demanding, and have expensive tastes.

✓Mars in Gemini ♊
Someone who may not want to become too deeply or emotionally involved with any one partner. A strong sexual desire is unusual, but there is great liking for innovation, variety and change in the style of love-making; many lovers are likely, with relationships kept at a superficial level.

Mars in Cancer ♋
Highly sexed, but nevertheless roughness and boisterousness will be intensely disliked, so a gentle and sensitive approach is most advisable. Very strong feelings, emotions and intuitions are always present, and there is a tendency to cling to a relationship. In Cancer, Mars often increases fertility.

Mars in Leo ♌
Mars in Leo appreciates comfort and luxurious, aesthetically pleasing surroundings for sexual activities, and the result could be a highly sophisticated romp. There should undoubtedly be plenty of lively response to advances, but a slight hint of con-

descension may make one feel like an ever-grateful subject!

Mars in Virgo ♍

Virgo is purity personified, but Mars is all energy and sex: a contradiction in terms. Desire is certainly present, but the expression of it in a straightforward way may not be at all easy. Psychological difficulties as a result of conflict can cause repression, and deviation is possible.

Mars in Libra ♎

A languid attitude towards sex is very likely, and excuses may be made to put off the over-ardent lover. Once aroused, sensuousness will be evident; but, even so, sex has to be idealistic, colorful and beautiful—"out of this world" rather than earthy!

Mars in Scorpio ♏

Mars in Scorpio, more than in any other Sign, will make the individual extremely highly sexed. Unfortunately, jealousy and resentfulness can frequently blight relationships. Possibly the best way to combat this is to cultivate demanding interests, so that the excess of energy and emotion is positively directed.

Mars in Sagittarius ♐

A lively, unserious attitude to sex is likely. The man or woman with Mars in Sagittarius will enjoy relationships, but will make and break them easily, for freedom is highly prized. Those with Mars in Sagittarius will be passionate, but the grass will always seem greener on the other side!

Mars in Capricorn ♑

If those with Mars in Capricorn, caught up in the essential business of getting on in the world, can find the time to indulge in sexual relationships, they will be seething with passion at one moment, and an iceberg the next; but they will admire and identify with faithfulness and constancy.

Mars in Aquarius ♒

Having an affair with someone with Mars in Aquarius will be an interesting experience, but togetherness, in the physical sense, may seem almost a necessary evil to them! They accept the fact that desires must be satisfied, but are somehow "above it all"; passion is not really their scene.

Mars in Pisces ♓

Passion must always be combined with a colorful romanticism for those with Mars in Pisces. The emotional level is extremely high, but plain and simple earthy pleasures may not be enough to satisfy some highly individual escapist tendencies. An uncomplicated "strong" partner will have a beneficial steadying influence.

Mars chart

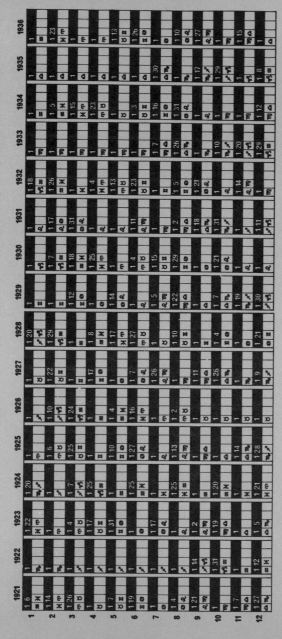

Mars chart

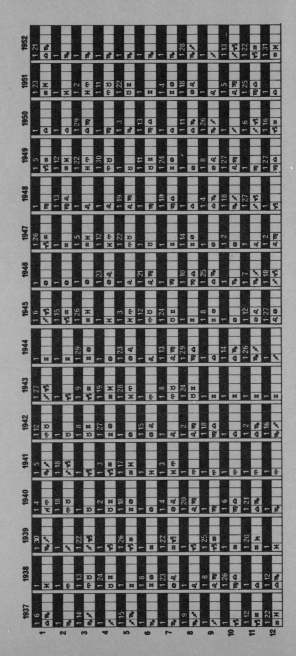

Mars chart

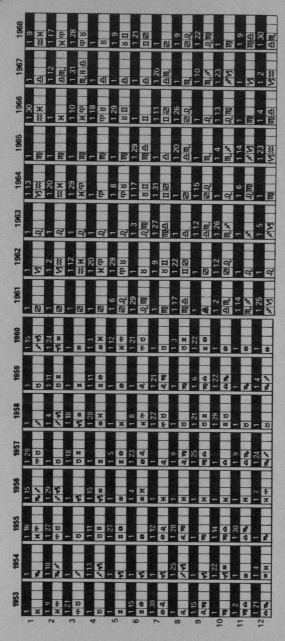